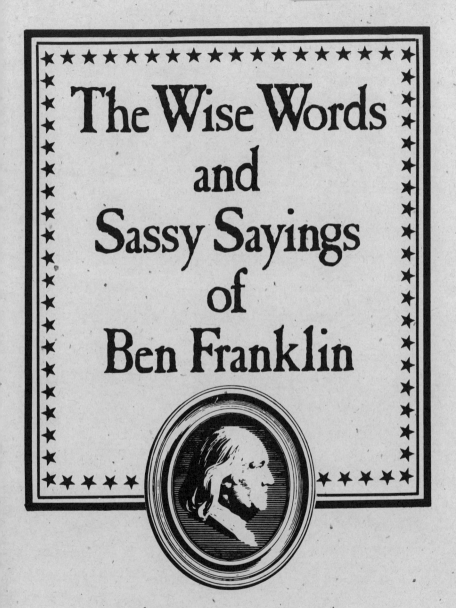

The Wise Words and Sassy Sayings of Ben Franklin

Franklin Savings and Loan Association
Home Office: Eighth and Market Streets, San Francisco
Branch Offices: Danville, Geneva-Mission (S. F.), Larkspur,
Pleasanton (2), San Jose (2), San Mateo, and Santa Rosa

The American Sage

On January 17, 1706, a tenth son was born to a poor Boston candle-maker. He was named Benjamin Franklin. Needless to say, the family could not afford a formal education for Ben. But that did not stand in his way at all. Ben devised many unique ways to gain knowledge—even becoming a vegetarian to save money for buying books.

Because of his love for books, he entered the printing trade. And in twenty short years he made his fortune and retired at the age of 42 to devote his life to scientific study and "to doing good."

Among his many publishing ventures, Ben Franklin wrote an annual almanac under the pseudonym of Richard Saunders. *Poor Richard's Almanack* became a best seller and a great influence upon the moral and social habits of his day. A brief version of the 25 almanacs was put into a single volume called *The Way to Wealth*. This was translated into a dozen languages and became a best seller in North America and Europe alike.

The series of *Poor Richard* almanacs, published between 1732 and 1757, contained famous maxims encouraging thrift, industry and other virtuous modes of behavior. But contrary to popular belief, these maxims were not all original sayings from the fertile mind of Ben Franklin. In fact, a good percent of the Poor Richard Sayings came from collections of proverbs and epigrams of the Old World, but Americanized by Franklin's hand.

To this day, we are still influenced by such sayings as "Waste not, want not," "Early to bed, early to rise, makes a man healthy, wealthy and wise." This booklet is just a small sampling of Poor Richard Sayings which have been passed down from generation to generation. You'll find some sober, some witty, some trite, and some sassy and happy; but you'll find them all imbued with a grain of wisdom that has kept them alive for so many years.

Many people will claim that Ben Franklin's greatest influence upon America and the world were these almanacs. But a little delving into history will show otherwise. This giant of an American lived such a creative and forward looking life that his many accomplishments still influence our everyday lives, even though we do not give him the credit for it.

It would be impossible in this short space to name all his wonderful achievements, so a brief listing must suffice. Ben Franklin's proof of his electricity principle, using a kite to attract lightning, led eventually to the electric motor, telephone and telegraph. He invented the lightning rod, bifocal lenses, glass harmonica, library chair, and of course, the Franklin stove. And who can escape daylight saving time or the postal service? Ben instigated both and was even the country's first Postmaster General.

He edited the most successful newspaper in the American colonies; drew the first newspaper cartoon; founded the first circulating library; and established the first chartered fire insurance company in America. Even the weather did not escape his vibrant mind. He is the Father of the U.S. Weather Bureau.

Although Ben had his share of aches and pains, he remained vigorous to his very last days. At the age of 81, he attended daily sessions of the Constitutional Convention to convince and urge all factions to sign the Constitution. This great diplomat's last public service was to urge ratification of the Constitution and the approval and inauguration of the new government under his colleague, George Washington.

What exactly was Ben Franklin? A philosopher, diplomat, scientist, meteorologist, inventor, economist, humorist, printer, mason, athlete, soldier, writer, or businessman? He was all these and more. One could call him a "Renaissance Man" who was not only able to dream, but was able to fulfill those dreams.

It is obvious from his accomplishments that Ben practiced what he preached. And it is our hope at Franklin Savings that this small sampling of wise words and sassy sayings will bring you many moments of guidance, encouragement, entertainment and smiles.

Thrift

Beware of little expenses;
A small leak will sink a great ship.

For age and want, save while you may,
No morning sun lasts a whole day.

Get what you can, and what you get hold;
'Tis the stone that will turn all your lead into gold.

Buy what thou hast no need of,
and ere long thou shalt sell thy necessaries.

At a great pennyworth pause a while.

'Tis foolish to lay out money in a purchase of repentance.

Silks and satins, scarlets and velvets put out the kitchen fire.

Think of saving as well as of getting.

Who dainties love, shall beggars prove.

When the well's dry, they know the worth of water.

Great estates may venture more,
But little boats should keep near shore.

'Tis a well spent penny that saves a groat.

A penny saved is two pence clear.
A pin a-day is a groat a-year. Save and have.

Every little makes a mickle.

He that buys by the penny, maintains not only himself, but other people.

Dine with little, sup with less:
Do better still, sleep supperless.

Great Spenders are bad Lenders.

Light Purse, heavy Heart.

All things are cheap to the saving,
dear to the wasteful.

When Prosperity was well mounted, she let go the Bridle and soon came tumbling out of the Saddle.

The thrifty maxim of the wary Dutch,
is to save all the money they can touch.

Rather go to bed supperless than run in debt for a Breakfast.

Waste not, Want not.

Borrowing

If you would know the value of money, go and try to borrow some.

He that goes a borrowing, goes a sorrowing.

The second vice is lying,
the first is running into debt.

Lying rides upon debt's back.

Creditors are a superstitious sect,
great observers of set days and times.

Creditors have better memories than debtors.

Those have a short Lent who owe money to be paid at Easter.

Rather go to bed supperless than rise in debt.

Lend money to an Enemy, and thou'lt gain him;
to a Friend, and thou'lt lose him.

Pay who you owe, and you'll know what is your own.

Time

Haste makes Waste.

But dost thou love life? Then do not squander time, for that's the stuff life is made of.

Lost time is never found again.

He that riseth late must trot all day, and shall scarce overtake his business at night; while laziness travels so slowly that Poverty soon overtakes him.

Early to bed and early to rise
Makes a man healthy, wealthy, and wise.

One to-day is worth two to-morrows.

Have you somewhat to do to-morrow? Do it to-day!

Constant dropping wears away stones.

Employ thy time well, if thou meanest to gain leisure.

Since thou art not sure of a minute, throw not away an hour!

Fear not Death; for the sooner we die,
the longer shall we be immortal.

Wish not so much to live long, as to live well.

If you have time, don't wait for Time.

Tomorrow I'll reform,
The fool does say;
Today itself's too late—
The wise did yesterday.

Enjoy the present hour, be mindful of the past;
and neither fear nor wish the approaches of the
last.

You may delay, but Time will not.

Sudden Power is apt to be insolent, sudden Liberty
saucy; that behaves best which has grown gradually.

Time is an herb that cures all diseases.

He that can have Patience can have what he will.

A Child thinks 20 Shillings and 20 Years can scarce
ever be spent.

Prodigality of Time produces Poverty of Mind as
well as of Estate.

Wisdom

Great Good-nature, without Prudence, is a great Misfortune.

The family of Fools is ancient.

Experience keeps a dear school, yet Fools will learn in no other.

You will be careful, if you are wise, how you touch men's Religion, or Credit, or Eyes.

The heart of the Fool is in his mouth, but the mouth of the wise is in his heart.

There's none deceived but he that trusts.

The most exquisite Folly is made of Wisdom spun too fine.

Life with Fools consists in Drinking; with the wise Man, living's Thinking.

The wise Man draws more Advantage from his Enemies, than the Fool from his Friends.

Tim was so learned, that he could name a Horse in nine Languages. So ignorant, that he bought a Cow to ride on.

At 20 years of age the will reigns; at 30 the wit; at 40 the judgment.

The Things which hurt, instruct.

If Passion drives, let Reason hold the Reins.

To err is human, to repent divine; to persist devilish.

Take counsel in Wine, but resolve afterwards in Water.

Wise Men learn by others' harms; Fools by their own.

Would you persuade, speak of interest, not of reason.

Samson, for all his strong Body, had a weak Head, or he would not have laid it in a Harlot's lap.

It is wise not to seek a Secret and honest not to reveal it.

Honesty

Avoid dishonest gain: no price can recompense the pangs of vice.

What you would seem to be, be really.

Tricks and treachery are the practice of Fools that have not wit enough to be honest.

None but the well-bred Man knows how to confess a fault, or acknowledge himself in an error.

Mankind are very odd Creatures: One half censure what they practise, the other half practise what they censure; the rest always say and do as they ought.

The Sting of a Reproach is the Truth of it.

The Wise and Brave dares own that he was wrong.

Silence and Secrecy

Those who in Quarrels interpose,
Must often wipe a bloody Nose.

The worst wheel of the cart makes the most noise.

Well done is better than well said.

A Pair of good Ears will wring dry an hundred Tongues.

He that would live in peace and at ease, must not speak all he knows, nor judge all he sees.

Half Wits talk much but say little.

In a discreet man's mouth a publick thing is private.

E'er you remark another's sin, bid your own conscience look within.

Man's tongue is soft,
And bone doth lack;
Yet a stroke therewith
May break a man's back.

Proclaim not all thou knowest, all thou owest, all thou hast, nor all thou can'st.

You may talk too much on the best of Subjects.

Hear no ill of a Friend, nor speak any of an Enemy.

If you would keep your secret from an Enemy, tell it not to a Friend.

Let thy discontents be thy secrets;
—if the World know them 'twill despise thee and increase them.

Here comes Glib-Tongue; who can out-flatter a Dedication; and lie, like ten Epitaphs.

The Tongue offends, and the Ears get the cuffing.

Great talkers, little doers.

When man and woman die,
As poets sung
His heart's the last part moves,
Her last, the tongue.

A Slip of the Foot you may soon recover, but a slip of the Tongue you may never get over.

Teach your Child to hold his tongue, he'll learn fast enough to speak.

Three may keep a secret if two of them are dead.

Great Talkers should be cropp'd, for they have no need of Ears.

As we must account for every idle Word, so we must for every idle Silence.

To whom thy secret thou dost tell, to him thy freedom thou dost sell.

Silence is not always a Sign of Wisdom, but Babbling is ever a Folly.

Hunger

Eat few Suppers, and you'll need few Medicines.

At the working-man's house hunger looks in, but dares not enter.

There's many witty Men whose brains can't fill their bellies.

Where there is Hunger, Law is not regarded; and where Law is not regarded, there will be Hunger.

Hunger is the best Pickle.

Eat to live, and not live to eat.

To lengthen thy Life, lessen thy Meals.

Great famine when Wolves eat Wolves.

A full Belly is the Mother of all Evil.

Eating sour Pickles won't kill your Appetite.

Many Dishes, many Diseases.

I saw few die of hunger; of eating—100,000.

He that would travel much, should eat little.

Industry

If you would have your business done, go; if not, send.

God helps them that help themselves.

Sloth like rust, consumes faster than labor wears;
while the used key is always brighter.

The sleeping fox catches no poultry.

There will be sleeping enough in the grave.

Sloth makes all things difficult,
but industry all things easy.

Drive thy business! Let not that drive thee!

Industry need not wish.

He that lives on hope will die fasting.

Industry pays debts, while despair increaseth them.

Diligence is the Mother of good luck,
and God gives all things to industry.

Then plough deep while sluggards sleep,
And you shall have corn to sell and to keep.

By diligence and patience the mouse ate in two the
cable.

Little strokes fell great oaks.

Many, without labor, would live by their wits only, but they'll break for want of stock; whereas industry gives comfort, and plenty, and respect.

Keep thy shop, and they shop will keep thee.

He that by the plough would thrive,
Himself must either hold or drive.

The eye of the master will do more work than both his hands.

A little well-gotten will do us more good, than lordships and sceptres by Rapine and Blood.

He that hath a trade hath an estate, and he that hath a calling hath an office of profit and honor.

There are lazy Minds as well as lazy Bodies.

Industry, Perseverance, and Frugality, make Fortune yield.

O Lazy bones! Dost thou think God would have given thee arms and legs, if he had not designed thou should'st use them?

No Gains without Pains.

Be always ashamed to catch thyself idle.

He that waits upon Fortune, is never sure of a dinner.

Nothing humbler than Ambition, when it is about to climb.

The discontented Man finds no easy Chair.

All things are easy to Industry, all things difficult to Sloth.

Would you live with ease, do what you ought, not what you please.

Early to Bed and Early to Rise makes a Man healthy, wealthy, and wise.

Work as if you were to live 100 years, Pray as if you were to die tomorrow.

Friendship and Love

No better relation than a prudent and faithful Friend.

There are three faithful Friends—an old Wife, an old Dog, and ready Money.

If you would have Guests merry with cheer, be so yourself, or so at least appear.

Be slow in chusing a Friend, slower in changing.

Let all Men know thee, but no man know thee thoroughly: Men freely ford that see the shallows.

Monkeys, warm with envious spite, their most obliging friends will bite.

An open Foe may prove a curse; But a pretended Friend is worse.

Tart Word make no Friends: a spoonful of honey will catch more flies than a Gallon of Vinegar.

Promises may get thee friends, but non-performance will turn them into enemies.

A true Friend is the best Possession.

The same man cannot be both Friend and Flatterer.

Friends are the true Sceptres of Princes.

He that lieth down with Dogs, shall rise up with Fleas.

There are no ugly loves, nor handsome prisons.

Where yet was ever found the mother,
who'd change her booby for another?

Love well, whip well.

Happy's the Wooing that's not long a doing.

Approve not of him who commends all you say.

Love and Tooth-ache have many Cures, but none infallible, except Possession and Disposession.

Do good to thy friend to keep him, to thy enemy to gain him.

Love your Neighbour; yet don't pull down your Hedge.

Friendship cannot live with Ceremony, nor without Civility.

Thou can'st not joke an Enemy into a Friend, but thou may'st a Friend into an Enemy.

26

He that sells upon Trust, loses many friends, and always wants money.

Friendship increases by visiting Friends, but by visiting seldom.

'Tis great Confidence in a Friend to tell him your Faults, greater to tell him his.

A Brother may not be a Friend,
but a Friend will always be a Brother.

Pride

Fond pride of dress is, sure, a very curse;
Ere fancy you consult, consult your purse.

Pride is as loud a beggar as Want,
and a great deal more saucy.

Pride that dines on vanity sups on contempt.

Pride breakfasted with Plenty,
dined with Poverty, and supped with Infamy.

The Devil wipes his Breech with poor Folks' Pride.

Declaiming against Pride, is not always a Sign of
Humility.

As Pride increases, Fortune declines.

Many complain of their Memory, few of their
Judgment.

He that cannot obey, cannot command.

Success has ruined many a Man.

Sally laughs at everything you say. Why? Because
she has fine teeth.

Poverty, poetry, and new titles of honour, make
men ridiculous.

The Proud hate Pride—in others.

On Various Human Frailties

Now I have a sheep and a cow,
Everybody bids me good morrow.

Want of care does us more damage than want of knowledge.

Not to oversee workmen is to leave them your purse open.

Power to the bold, and Heaven to the virtuous.

If you would have a faithful servant, and one that you like, serve yourself.

A little neglect may breed great mischief.

For want of a nail the shoe was lost;
for want of a shoe, the horse was lost;
and for want of a horse the rider was lost.

A man may keep his nose all his life to the grindstone, and die not worth a groat at last.

A fat kitchen makes a lean will.

Women and wine, game and deceit,
Make the wealth small and the wants great.

What maintains one vice would bring up two children.

Fools make feasts, and wise men eat them.

A ploughman on his legs is higher than a gentleman on his knees.

'Tis easier to suppress the first desire,
than to satisfy all that follow it.

We may give advice, but we cannot give conduct.

Many a long dispute among Divines may be thus abridged, It is so; It is not so; It is so; It is not so.

Ill Customs and Bad Advice are seldom forgotten.

He that speaks ill of the Mare, will buy her.

How few there are who have courage enough to own their Faults, or resolution enough to mend them.

He that can compose himself, is wiser than he that composes books.

A country man between two lawyers, is like a Fish between two Cats.

A Traveller should have a Hog's nose, a Deer's legs, and an Ass's back.

There are more old Drunkards than old Doctors.

Harry Smatter, has a Mouth for every Matter.

Many Foxes grow grey, but few grow good.

Genius without Education is like Silver in the Mine.

You can bear your own Faults, why not a Fault in your Wife?

Doing an Injury puts you below your Enemy;
Revenging one makes you but even with him;
Forgiving it sets you above him.

An infallible Remedy for Toothache,
viz.—Wash the root of an aching Tooth, in Elder vinegar, and let it dry half an hour in the Sun; after which it will never ache more.

Beware, beware; he'll cheat without scruple, who can without fear.

The King's cheese is half wasted in parings; but no matter, 'tis made of the People's milk.

How many observe Christ's Birthday;
How few his Precepts!
O! 'tis easier to keep Holidays than Commandments.

A ship under sail and a big-bellied Woman, are the handsomest two things that can be seen common.

There is much difference between imitating a good man, and counterfeiting him.

'Tis easy to see, hard to foresee.

Caesar did not merit the triumphal car more than he that conquers himself.

Let thy maid-servant be faithful, strong, and homely.

Late Children, early Orphans.

Fish and Visitors stink after three days.

Quarrels never could last long,
If on one side only lay the wrong.

Strange! that a Man who has wit enough to write
a Satyr, should have folly enough to publish it.

Visit your Aunt, but not every Day;
and call at your Brother's but not every night.

Prayers and Provender hinder no journey.

An empty Bag cannot stand upright.

When you speak to a man, look on his eyes;
when he speaks to thee, look on his mouth.

Observe all men; thyself most.

A rich rogue is like a fat hog, who never does good
till as dead as a log.

If evils come not,
Then our fears are vain;
And if they do,
Fear but augments the pain.

Learn of the skillful: He that teaches himself, hath
a fool for his master.

Great beauty, great strength, and great riches are really and truly of no great use; a right Heart exceeds all.

To bear other people's afflictions, every one has courage enough to spare.

Epitaph on a Scolding Wife by her Husband:
Here my poor Bridget's Corps doth lie,
she is at rest, and so am I.

Ceremony is not Civility; nor is Civility Ceremony.

An undutiful Daughter will prove an unmanageable Wife.

Glass, China, and Reputation, are easily crack'd, and never well mended.

He is not well bred, that cannot bear Ill-Breeding in others.

He's a fool that makes his Doctor his Heir.

After three days men grow weary of a wench, a guest, and weather rainy.

He that drinks fast, pays slow.

The Bell calls others to Church, but itself never minds the Sermon.

The Morning Daylight appears plainer when you put out your Candle.

Search others for their Virtues, thyself for thy Vices.

Clean your Finger, before you point at my Spots.

Who is strong? He that can conquer his bad Habits.

A man in a Passion rides a mad Horse.

Fear to do ill, and you need fear nought else.

Seven wealthy towns contend for Homer dead,
Thro' which the living Homer beg'd his bread.

Marry above thy match, thou'lt get a master.

Seek Virtue, and of that possest,
To Providence resign the rest.

Tho' Modesty is a Virtue, Bashfulness is a Vice.

Hide not your Talents, they for Use were made:
"What's a Sun-Dial in the Shade?"

Wink at small faults—remember thou hast great ones.

Craft must be at charge for clothes, but Truth can go naked.

He that takes a Wife takes Care.

Full of Courtesie, full of Craft.

Neither a Fortress nor a Maidenhead will hold out long after they begin to parley.

Serving God is doing good to Man, but praying is thought an easier Service, and therefore more generally chosen.

Wealth is not his that has it, but his that enjoy it.

Men and melons are hard to know.

Keep your Mouth wet, Feet dry.

If you would reap Praise you must sow the Seeds, gentle Words and useful Deeds.

Many have quarrel'd about Religion, that never practised it.

If man could have Half his Wishes he would double his Troubles.

It is better to take many Injuries, than to give one.

To be humble to superiors is duty, to equals courtesy, to inferiors nobleness.

Do not do that which you would not have known.

Anger is never without a Reason, but seldom with a good One.

An ill Wound, but not an ill Name, may be healed.

A lean Award is better than a fat Judgment.

Light heel'd Mothers make leaden heel'd Daughters.

He that whines for Glass without G, take away L and that's he.

A quarrelsome Man has no good Neighbours.

Nothing brings more Pain than too much Pleasure; nothing more bondage than too much Liberty, (or Libertinism).

Don't throw stones at your neighbours', if your own windows are glass.

The Honey is sweet, but the Bee has a Sting.

Keep your eyes wide open before Marriage, half shut afterwards.

Why does the blind man's Wife paint herself?

Many a Man thinks he is buying Pleasure, when he is really selling himself a Slave to it.

There is no Man so bad but he secretly respects the Good.

Fly Pleasures, and they'll follow you.

If you do what you should not, you must hear what you would not.

He that scatters thorns, let him not go barefoot.

Most People return small Favours, acknowledge middling ones, and repay great ones with Ingratitude.

The Golden Age never was the present Age.

Death takes no Bribes.

'Tis more noble to forgive, and more manly to despise, than to revenge an Injury.

Man, dally not with other Folks' Women or Money.

An egg to-day is better than a hen to-morrow.

Tell a miser he's rich, and a woman she's old, you'll get no Money of one, nor Kindness of t'other.

The rotten Apple spoils his Companion.

Cunning proceeds from Want of Capacity.

What more valuable than Gold? Diamonds. Than Diamonds? Virtue.

The hasty Bitch brings forth blind Puppies.

A Change of Fortune hurts a wise Man no more than a Change of the Moon.

Fools need Advice most, but only wise Men are the better for it.

Nothing dries sooner than a tear.

Let thy Child's first lesson be obedience, and the second will be what thou wilt.

Blessed is he that expects nothing, for he shall never be disappointed.

Old Boys have their Playthings as well as young Ones; the Difference is only in the Price.

With the old Almanack and the old Year, Leave thy old Vices, 'tho' ever so dear.

The Thirteen Virtues:

1. Temperance: Eat not to dullness. Drink not to elevation.

2. Silence: Speak not but what may benefit others or yourself. Avoid trifling conversation.

3. Order: Let all your things have their places. Let each part of your business have its time.

4. Resolution: Resolve to perform what you ought. Perform without fail what you resolve.

5. Frugality: Make no expense but to do good to others or yourself, i.e., waste nothing.

6. Industry: Lose no time. Be always employed in something useful. Cut off all unnecessary actions.

7. Sincerity: Use no hurtful deceit. Think innocently and justly; if you speak, speak accordingly.

8. Justice: Wrong none by doing injuries or omitting the benefits that are your duty.

9. Moderation: Avoid extremes. Forbear resenting injuries so much as you think they deserve.

10. Cleanliness: Tolerate no uncleanliness in body, clothes, or habitation.

11. Tranquility: Be not disturbed at trifles or at accidents common or unavoidable.

12. Chastity: Rarely use venery but for health or offspring—never to dullness, weakness, or the injury of your own or another's peace or reputation.

13. Humility: Imitate Jesus and Socrates.

The History of Franklin Savings

On November 18, 1875, Articles of Incorporation were filed by a thrift-minded group of German-Americans for a new corporation to be known as the Franklin Savings and Building Association. The Incorporators were: Otto Fauss, George Lang, Henry Habermahl, Henry B. Wagner, Joseph Kahn, Frederick Wickenhauser, Julius Thierbach, Hugo Pfersdorff, Jacob Dodge, F. J. Castelhun and S. Simmons, all of San Francisco. The first Officers were: President, Henry Habermahl; Vice President, George Lang; Treasurer, Otto Fauss; Secretary, Hugo Pfersdorff. The Association's first office was at 539 California Street.

Other early records of the Association are rather sketchy except that it is known that the Association was organized for a period of 50 years—"After which time the Association must disincorporate pursuant to law" according to the By-Laws. Another section of the By-Laws provided "The Association may disincorporate sooner if existing liabilities do not forbid it, provided ¾ of its members vote in favor of disincorporation. Disincorporation is accomplished by means of Judicial proceedings." The Association accumulated funds by issuing shares in series, not to exceed 3,000 per series, each with a maximum paid-in value of $200. Loans were made to the member bidding the most interest in advance at an auction.

Another provision of the By-Laws was that "The meetings may be conducted in German or English but the Minutes must be written in German." The foregoing By-Law conditions were very important to the early members of Franklin, as it represented the continuation of their German heritage.

According to the records that are available, the Association grew very slowly for, as was the case with most building and loan

43

associations, it was only a part-time interest of the Directors, and the Manager, usually known as the Secretary, devoted only a portion of his time to the Association's activities.

Meetings of the association were generally held in the evenings and dues on the shares were paid at each meeting. A system of fines was invoked if members did not pay the dues on their shares promptly.

In 1895, the Association's office was 413 Bush street and in 1900 was 10 O'Farrell street. For a period of 31 years, Franklin Savings and Building Association operated without any extraordinary happenings, until on April 18, 1906 when disaster struck in the form of earthquake and fire that practically leveled downtown San Francisco. This included the building at 10 O'Farrell Street housing the Odeon Cafe owned by Director Adolf Becker, in which building Franklin Savings and Building Association had occupied a room as its meeting place. Shortly before the earthquake and fire a new Secretary, B. J. H. Fedde, had been appointed in place of William Hatje who died in March, 1906. During the course of the earthquake and fire, practically all of the Association's records were destroyed with the exception of a cash book found at the home of William Hatje in Alameda. This naturally created a great problem with the Association. On May 3, 1906, the Directors called a meeting to decide what action to take. Present at this meeting were: J. F. C. Ludemann, Philip Kiefer, C. G. Meussdorffer, Otto Lang, August Lang, August Jungblut, Charles Schlesinger and B. Fedde. Directors P. F. Rathjens and F. Eickhorst were not present. The President in 1906 was J. F. C. Ludemann who was elected to that post in 1891. He was one of the Charter Members in 1875; however, not one of the Incorporators. After the 1906 disaster, the Association met for a while at 1508 Ellis Street. There was a great deal of discussion about what should be done inasmuch as the Association's records were destroyed and a vote was taken on June 11, 1906 of all members to determine whether they wished to withdraw or remain with the Association. The majority of the members decided to remain and to continue in business.

All of the minutes were written in German according to the old

44

By-Laws and the German minutes even went so far as to translate the legal name of the Association, Franklin Savings and Building Association into German which read: "Franklin Spar Und Bau Verein." It was then decided that the only way of perpetuating the institution, restoring the Association's records and organizing the Association on more modern lines, was to reincorporate. So on October 18, 1906 the Directors passed a resolution "RESOLVED, that this Corporation give its consent to the incorporation of the Franklin Mutual Building and Loan Association and to the issuance by the Secretary of State to said Franklin Mutual Building and Loan Association Articles of Incorporation."

The incorporators of the new Association were: J. F. C. Ludemann, August Lang, Adolf Becker, Philip Kiefer, August H. Jungblut, F. G. Eickhorst, Charles Schlesinger, P. F. Rathjens, B. J. H. Fedde and F. J. Castelhun, who was the Association's attorney. Mr. Castelhun had a long career with Franklin, having been the attorney who prepared the original Articles of Incorporation in 1875. He continued as the Association's attorney for many years thereafter.

Following the issuance of the Articles of Incorporation for Franklin Mutual Building and Loan Association the new Association organized for business on November 6, 1906 at 1343 Golden Gate Avenue, San Francisco, which had been the address of the Franklin Savings and Building Association. The officers then elected were: J. F. C. Ludemann, President; August J. Lang, Vice President; B. J. H. Fedde, Secretary. The new Association took over the Assets and Liabilities of the former Franklin Savings and Building Association which finally wound up its affairs at a meeting held on May 14, 1907.

J. F. C. Ludemann served as President until his death in 1912 terminating 37 years with the Association. B. J. H. Fedde served as Secretary from 1906 until his retirement in 1944; he died in 1953.

In 1943, the name of Franklin Mutual Building and Loan Association was dropped and the present name of Franklin Savings and Loan Association was adopted. The Association was one of the first in California to apply for insurance of accounts in 1935.

Many changes have taken place in the Savings and Loan Industry since 1875. Upstairs offices have been replaced by substantial buildings; part-time offices and personnel have become full time operations with trained staffs; old hand-bookkeeping systems are now computerized. Franklin Savings has progressed with the entire savings and loan business.

In 1964, the headquarters office of the Association moved to a new building on the corner of Eighth and Market streets in San Francisco. The handsome white marble building, of classic architecture, is a landmark on upper Market street.

Franklin continued its expansion in 1969 by opening its first branch—an office located in Danville. This was shortly followed by a merger with the Nucleus Building and Loan Association of San Jose, another veteran savings and loan firm, founded in 1889. In 1972, Franklin opened its fourth office in the thriving Alameda County city of Pleasanton.

Over two hundred years ago, Ben Franklin entered this familiar maxim in his Poor Richard's Almanack:
> "Great oaks from little
> acorns grow."

Franklin Savings, in nearly a century of service to California, has followed the ancient adage of its namesake, the man whose collection of pithy proverbs is here presented for your enjoyment.

Type used in this book is set in Caslon Antique and Trump Medieval (Fototronic set). Paper stock is Kilmory 1776 for the inside pages and Torino for the Cover. Lithographed in San Francisco by Kohnke Printing Company. Illustrations courtesy of The Bettman Archives.